Nick Cave
On the Fragility of Life

ERIS
gems

SINCE THE LATE NINETEEN-SEVENTIES, the Australian musician Nick Cave has given voice to our gnarliest impulses and fears. As a founding member of the cacophonous post-punk band the Birthday Party, he sang of sexual perversions and violent reveries in a dank baritone, a misfit visionary in the spirit of Tom Waits, Alan Vega, and Iggy Pop. (In 1981, "Release the Bats," one of the band's first singles—"Release the bats! Release the bats! Pump them up and explode the things!"—was declared Song of the Year by the BBC broadcaster John Peel.) In 1983, Cave formed Nick Cave and the Bad Seeds; over time, his lyrics grew sharper and more striking. In 1997, he released "The Boatman's Call," a bleak and tender piano record about romantic devastation. The album showcases his aptitude for articulating heavy and complex human experiences with elegance and gall. If you have ever felt a strange, throbbing ache somewhere low in your gut—born of heartbreak, yearning, or some depraved desire—Cave probably has a song for that.

In 2015, when Cave was fifty-seven, his fifteen-year-old son, Arthur, died after accidentally falling from a cliff near the family's home, in Brighton, England. In the aftermath, Cave turned his focus to another taboo experience: grief. "Skeleton Tree" (2016), the first record he released following Arthur's death, opens with a declaration: "You fell from the sky, crash-landed in a field near the River Adur," he chants. "With my voice, I am calling you." The album was followed, in 2019, by "Ghosteen," a singular and profound meditation on loss and the afterlife. I have never heard anything like it. On "Bright Horses," Cave occasionally breaks into a pure, spectral falsetto that sounds only partially human. "Everyone has a heart, and it's calling for something," he sings in an early verse.

Through these records and his long-running newsletter, "The Red Hand Files," Cave has become an unexpected Virgil for anyone mired in grief and casting about for a warm but unsentimental guide. His advice is compassionate and perceptive. (To a man who lost his cousin, and whose aunt now appears entirely subsumed by her grief, he counsels only patience. "Aunt Marnie is spending time with the retreating image of her departed son and perhaps there is no room for you at this moment. Perhaps now is not the time she needs you, but you can be sure, in time, she will," he writes.) In 2018, Cave announced a series of tour dates in which he would be in conversation with his audience, a format he described as being about "intimacy and connectedness." Last year, he published "Faith, Hope and Carnage," an extended interview with the journalist Seán O'Hagan; a paperback version will be released by Picador in September. Cave has been open about his suffering, even as it changes shape. In 2022, seven years after Arthur's death, Cave's oldest son, Jethro, died in Melbourne at age thirty-one. (Cave is currently married to the British model and designer Susie Cave; Jethro was the child of an earlier relationship, with Beau Lazenby.)

"I'm not talking about Jethro, because his mother has expressly asked me not to," Cave told me recently. "She's a grieving mother and very protective over him."

When I lost my husband suddenly, this past August, Cave's late-career albums were some of the only music I could tolerate. Though it is a brutally common experience, grief is still challenging to evoke or explain. In those early weeks, I often listened to "Ghosteen" after putting my baby daughter to bed, finding comfort in its wildness and mystery. Our conversation, which took place first over the phone and later over e-mail, has been condensed and edited.

Nick, thanks for taking the time to talk with me.

I'm a little agitated, to be honest. I forgot about the interview! I've been in songwriting mode, writing lyrics. Excuse me if I'm a little scattered. But let's give it a go. Before we start, Amanda, I'm truly sorry to hear about your husband.

Thank you. I wanted to tell you that your work has been a guiding light for me through my grief, an experience that I have found mostly bewildering. I often feel as though I'm not in the best place for a conversation, either. Yet here we are!

And yet here we are.

I was rereading "Faith, Hope and Carnage" while preparing to speak with you today, and on the very first page you say, "Interviews, in general, suck. Really. They eat you up. I hate them." That made me laugh. Often I hate them, too.

Yes, they can take so much away. Especially music interviews. You make a record and love it until you start talking about it in interviews. You suck the life out of it, strip it of any mystery that it may have had. I just don't like the process. It's ironic because, for "Faith, Hope and Carnage," I ended up speaking to Seán O'Hagan for fifty hours, or something like that. But it was well understood that I didn't want to talk about music in particular, and that I didn't want to talk about my life in a conventional way. We were able to talk about other things. Since doing this, I have come to see the interview as almost an art form in itself. I found out, to my bewilderment and amazement, that interviews, or conversations, could actually be a way of communicating! [Laughs.] I'd never really considered an interview to be that before.

I found that the back-and-forth between you and Seán left space for doubt, wondering, doubling back. Traditional interviews, traditional memoirs, they can feel so closed and declarative. Good conversation should have air in it.

That's a lovely way to put it. I think the conversation Seán and I had was much more about searching. Both of us were trying to work out where we stood in the world at that particular time, and what we thought about things. Throughout the interviews, my ideas kept shifting all the time.

I once interviewed the writer and environmentalist Wendell Berry, who was adamant about the importance of conversation to humanity's survival. He said, "It's either that or kill each other."

That's exactly right. It seems to be essential, even if just as a corrective for the bad, unexpressed ideas we hold in our heads. A lot of things I talked to Seán about I had never expressed before. They were thoughts and ideas that lived in my head. Grief. Religion. When we rehearse our ideas in our minds, it's always at a kind of fever pitch, and the ideas can feel extraordinarily articulate. But, once you actually hear yourself speak them, these ideas can appear considerably less robust, at least for me. Seán would ask me a question, and I'd say, "No, no, no." Then, a week later, he would circle around and ask the same question, and I'd say, "Yes. Yes, yes." It was in the process of talking about these matters that I came to a more considered, nuanced position on things. That's the beauty of the book, I think—that the conversation unfolds in real time, and we see before our eyes the power of conversation to develop and deepen ideas.

There's a moment early on in the book, just a page or two in, where you say, with some purpose, that the death of your son defines you. That sort of seismic, sudden, life-altering loss—for me, it feels like not only the only thing that has ever happened to me but also the only thing that has ever happened. I felt relief when you just declared it like that.

Yes, I just didn't recognize myself anymore. Did you feel the same way? I would look in the mirror and not really know who was staring back. I just seemed like a different kind of being. Grief is extraordinary in its capacity to completely alter us on an almost atomic level. Suddenly, we inhabit a different body. Our relationship with everything seems to change. It's as if we're simply a different person. I meant that quite literally. I changed from one person to another person.

People often comment on your willingness to engage directly with grief, first via the Conversations tour, and then with your writing of "The Red Hand Files"—you are uncommonly generous in this regard. Grief can feel burdensome for everyone, and yet I have also found that not engaging with it can be so lonesome.

Yes, I have found that, but, on the other hand, I didn't want to talk about it endlessly with friends. I found a basic acknowledgment of the situation went a long way. In the book, I talk about the first time I went out in public after my son died and a woman from Infinity Foods, a vegetarian takeaway I used to go to, whom I knew. She didn't mention anything when she took my order, didn't say anything, which I felt was strange, you know? But when she gave me back my change she squeezed my hand. It was a silent but deeply articulate act, beyond words, and more comforting than anything I had read or that anyone had said. It struck me that it doesn't require much for people to deal with the grief of others. It just requires a small, sincere acknowledgment, and then we can move on a little bit rather than be stuck alone in an undeclared falseness. But I do also understand that it can be very difficult for people to have to deal with somebody else's grief, especially if they are seeing them all the time.

I think people who are in the throes of fresh grief very quickly become hyperaware of the immovability of that feeling. The way it just kind of sits there.

Exactly. I read a beautiful line by the poet Ellen Bass, in a poem about grief called "The Thing Is." She says, "Grief weights you down like your own flesh / only more of it, an obesity of grief." That was quite a startling but deeply familiar image. Grief squeezes the common oxygen out of the room so that no one has air to breathe.

You have found a way to apply useful, elegant language to the experience of loss—

to articulate it with grace and accuracy. In the book, you describe the early days of your grief as "a place of acute disorder—a chaos that was also a kind of incapacitation." But you also point out that it's ordinary: "We are all, at some point in our lives, obliterated by loss." How did you build a vocabulary to describe these things?

For me, it became essential to work out a way of doing that. I needed a way to articulate grief. I did the in-conversation events, which, to me, were a not always successful attempt at expressing these things. I don't know really what I was trying to do when I did those; I'd gone a bit mad. They were strange things to do. So it was really with "The Red Hand Files" that I learned how to write about it—even though I couldn't really talk about it, at least I could develop a language around grief. It took the conversations with Seán—and they were sometimes quite painful—to work out, over time, a way of adequately describing the mechanics of grief. Seán allowed me the time, the room. We are often hyperconscious of the way our grief makes others feel. We become like antimatter sucking everything into the vacuum of our anguish, the air, the life. I don't know. I just found it difficult to talk normally to people about it. I had to work out a way where I could talk about it without driving myself and everyone else crazy. It's easier to talk to you about these sorts of things, Amanda, because I know you're in, as they say, "the club." The club no one wants to be in.

Has your relationship to violent imagery, either within or beyond your own work, changed at all in the last few years?

Yes, actually. There are things that Susie and I can't watch on the TV. Sometimes it seems like every second series on Netflix revolves around the loss or death of a child. We sit down together, and it's, like, "Oh, God. Here we go again." That kind of stuff is difficult. I wouldn't say I've lost my appetite for, say, violent literature or violent movies, though a lot of them seem kind of puerile these days. Maybe I'm just older. I hate to say this, to be honest, but I have found myself increasingly offended by movies that continuously and relentlessly involve the violent death of women. This might sound strange coming from me, given the kind of songs that I've written in the past, but I've lost my appetite for that. But, you know, there are little triggers, bits of catastrophic language or unforeseen, merciless reminders that exist within even the most benign movies. Susie and I have become deeply sensitized to each other's triggers. I won't go into detail—but these little devastations happen all the time. Susie and I are resilient. We've grown tough. But at the same time it doesn't take much to suddenly and momentarily destroy us.

The book also broaches the idea of religion and spirituality. At one point, you present music itself as a kind of argument against atheism. You describe it as "the great indicator that something else is going on, something unexplained, because it allows us to experience genuine moments of transcendence." Plenty of neurologists have prodded this idea—that humans have a kind of innate musicality—but, in my limited understanding of the research, it remains relatively hard to explain, on a physiological or evolutionary level, why music works on us.

My belief in God—well, that's a little complicated. I'm full of doubt in that respect, but replete with belief, too. Full of both things. Mostly, I inhabit a space between belief and unbelief. But, look, even if it turns out there is no actual divine dimension, music feels touched by something else. The creative process—especially original creation, which, for me, is writing words and music—can feel like hard labor and much of the time is as far away from anything you might call spiritual. I find it can be an agonizing and debilitating and solitary business. But there are sudden mystifying moments of spiritual freedom, where I am lifted from my feelings of inadequacy and I am suddenly flying around the room like a giggling fool, rapturously transported. That's not just the creative process—that's life in general. We lead our common lives, but all around there are hunches and intimations and whisperings of something else. These small, softly spoken suggestions are enough for me to feel that there is some enigmatic otherness to be experienced, and that's where my belief lies.

I understand where atheists are coming from. But I think the relentless shutting down of the idea of the divine is, for me, just bad for the business of songwriting. It feels limiting and uncreative. I think that many musicians are more prone to spiritual ideas because they are naturally closer to the mysterious act of creation. It's part of our occupation to inhabit a place that is at least adjacent to these ideas. So many musicians I know have a sort of unspoken, unannounced spirituality, which they experience naturally through the making of music.

That can happen through deep listening, too, I think. One thing you said earlier, and this comes up in the book also, is the faulty idea that doubt somehow precludes faith—that you can't have both doubt and faith at the same time. Yet maybe the act of balancing the two is the act of religiosity?

Yeah, I totally agree with that. I totally agree with myself. [Laughs.] But, of course, I don't think anyone who is serious about these matters doesn't doubt on some level. And, at the very least, doubt is the antidote to dogma and fanaticism and reductionism. This position—and this is not just a religious point of view; I would say, personally at least, this is where I sit on most things—is a place of uncertainty. This uncertainty or unknowing, which I equate with creativity, comes from an understanding of loss. We understand that life is not stable or dependable. This doubt feeds into everything I feel spiritually. I try to approach these matters with humility and uncertainty and to not be dogmatic. That's my problem with militant atheists: their lack of humility. But, in the end, I don't think atheism is the real problem. The atheist's point of view is weirdly sustained through the imagination of other people and their beliefs. A demoralized indifference to spiritual matters is the problem.

You're right that profound grief quickly pushes you away from both certitude and indifference, which are unproductive feelings—

That's right. Certitude and indifference. They're the problems with this world.

Am I asking too many questions about grief? I have found it to be an excruciating but nonetheless fascinating experience.

We have to be careful with that, because it drives people away. I mean that also on a professional level. Sadly, grief has its sell-by date, to some degree—not to the person who is grieving but to other people. We are expected to just get on with things. One of the reasons I keep doing "The Red Hand Files," week after week, is that people often write in to talk about losing someone and the very real pain they're in. . . . I'm sorry, this is quite difficult for me to talk about. Suddenly, you realize, Hang on, the person they are mourning died, like, fifteen years ago. It is extremely moving.

Because grief doesn't just go away. You become more resilient; you become more effective at navigating and dealing with your feelings. Yet the fundamental loss remains—it doesn't just dissipate—and, in a strange way, I think it can become a magnet for other losses. We come to see we are all simply creatures carrying around our ever-deepening loss. Small griefs seem to collect around the bigger primary grief. I think this realization allows us to become a true human being.

And I don't think this situation resolves itself as you grow older. In fact, more people just die. Loss becomes the primary condition of living. That doesn't mean you're in a hopeless, grief-stricken state all the time; it just means that you carry a deeper understanding of what it is to be human. We suffer as human beings, but out of that can come enormous joys, and genuine happiness, too. It can run in tandem with this ordinary sense of suffering. Otherwise, joy doesn't resonate fully. Joy seems to leap forth out of suffering. Regardless of your loss, you see how beautiful, how meaningful, how joyful the world can suddenly be. Human beings in general, you know, are fleeting things. That's something to understand on a fundamental level. That we have value. That we are precious.

You had a wonderful response to a fan sending you a song produced by ChatGPT "in the style of Nick Cave." You wrote, "This song sucks." Perhaps A.I. can never understand the sublime, or the self-annihilation, required to make good art.

When you see technology used in this way, does it make you concerned, or, conversely, could ChatGPT's inability to write a good song somehow help us value creative work more?

My objection is not with A.I. in general. For better or for worse, we are inextricably immersed in A.I. It is more a kind of sad, disappointed feeling that there are smart people out there that actually think the artistic act is so mundane that it can be replicated by a machine. I find that insulting. There's no earthly reason why we need to invent a technology that can mimic this most beautiful and mysterious creative act. Particularly writing a song. The thing about writing a good song is that it tells you something about yourself you didn't already know. That's the thing. You can't mimic that. The good song is always rushing forward. It annihilates, to some degree, the songs that you'd previously written, because you are moving forward all the time. That's what the creative impulse is—it's both creative and destructive and is always one step ahead of you. These impulses can't be replicated by a machine. Maybe A.I. can make a song that's indistinguishable from what I can do. Maybe even a better song. But, to me, that doesn't matter—that's not what art is. Art has to do with our limitations, our frailties, and our faults as human beings. It's the distance we can travel away from our own frailties. That's what is so awesome about art: that we deeply flawed creatures can sometimes do extraordinary things. A.I. just doesn't have any of that stuff going on. Ultimately, it has no limitations, so therefore can't inhabit the true transcendent artistic experience. It has nothing to transcend! It feels like such a mockery of what it is to be human. A.I. may very well save the world, but it can't save our souls. That's what true art is for. That's the difference. So, I don't know, in my humble opinion ChatGPT should just fuck off and leave songwriting alone.

You recently announced a new solo North American tour, featuring just you and the bassist Colin Greenwood, of Radiohead. I'm curious how you think about the practice of writing and recording versus performance?

It is genuinely difficult to sit down, with all your human limitations, and write a song. I am writing the lyrics to a new record at the moment, so all this is extremely raw, and I may be a little sensitive about these matters, to say the least! [Laughs.] But, as the months drag on, you slowly draw the small threads of ideas together that hopefully, eventually, make up a group of songs that become an album. Once you've got that done, things start to reveal themselves and make sense, and you go into the studio with your band members, and you start recording the music, and it's like collecting treasure. By the time you get these songs onto the stage, they have grown immensely in emotional stature. It can be a truly transcendent experience. So it's a beautiful, upward journey, to write songs and present them onstage. These small, wretched, little lines that you've clawed out of yourself are suddenly amplified onstage, by the brilliance of the musicians who play them, to the absolute delight of your audience. It's an extraordinary feeling, really, the trajectory of a small, inconsequential idea to something of true importance.

Anyway, I'm coming over to the States to promote "Faith, Hope and Carnage" when it comes out in paperback, because I didn't really get a chance to do anything in America when it was first published. And, at the same time, I'll be driving from town to town playing live shows, playing the piano, and singing in theatres and bringing Colin Greenwood along to play bass. He just fits in there and plays so beautifully.

Do you think this collaboration with Colin might extend to recording together?

We're making a Bad Seeds record soon. We haven't gone into the actual recording of it, but we have a brilliant bass player in the Bad Seeds, Martyn Casey. Marty lives in Perth, Australia, but maybe Colin will come in and play something. He has a completely different style from Marty. Marty's a jaw-dropping powerhouse who holds everything together. Colin tends to be more fluid and melodic.

Last month saw the tenth anniversary of "Push the Sky Away," which was also when you first began writing with Warren Ellis, a longtime collaborator in other roles. For me, there's something really special—something surreal, almost terrifying, yet so beautiful, too—about the albums you've made together. Can you talk a little bit about that relationship and how it has evolved over the years?

"Push the Sky Away" was a big moment in the direction of the band. Things changed completely. Part of that was a developing creative relationship with Warren. Warren Ellis, in case there is anyone out there who doesn't know, is a flat-out genius and general chaos-maker and a wonderful late-career creative partner to have found. So the process of songwriting became quite different, mostly in that we started to write the music to songs together as a team rather than me writing them by myself, as I have traditionally done. This re-energized things. So the past ten years have been extraordinarily creative. Amazing, really.

Warren has, to my enduring envy, an unflagging faith in his own abilities. Or at least he pretends to have it, which is part of the battle. This is extraordinarily helpful for someone like me, who suffers from a kind of chronic creative reticence. Warren can see, early on, the greatness in the small things. Those intimations! Those softly spoken ideas! It takes me a lot longer to establish a positive relationship with the things we write. So Warren is quite literally a gift.

Some artists talk about writing or making work as a kind of channelling. You have described the writing process as fraught and difficult, but has being onstage ever felt that way? As though you're receiving a signal?

For me, songwriting is essentially an office job: it's getting up in the morning, sitting down at nine o'clock, and working away at things. I'm not channelling, as such, or receiving these gifts flying down the spiritual pipeline, "the giant pencil from the sky," as Townes Van Zandt would say. But to perform onstage is another matter entirely. You can get reliably lost in a kind of circular, communal feeling of mutual regard with the audience—it's awesome—an incoming and outpouring of love that can only be called transcendent. You lose yourself completely, transform into something entirely different.

Anything that offers a kind of ego death, a moment of self-obliteration, can be—at least for me, in my grief, in my life—such a balm. Often, I just want to turn the volume down on myself a little bit.

Yes, that's right. Onstage, all external worries dissipate. There is no space for them. And of course it is like that with grief. There is no room for ordinary concerns. The great benefit of grief is, you develop a kind of audacity toward life in general, where it just doesn't fucking matter because the worst has happened. This is extremely freeing in its way. You do stuff that you wouldn't normally do because, well, what is the worst that can happen?

Suddenly, the world is full of radical possibility because you're not scared of anything anymore. It's kind of naïve, because you can always lose more, but it also feels very real.

Exactly. I find that it has made me bolder. I'm not so concerned with how I will be perceived, or what other people think of me. On an artistic level, there's more risk-taking. You lose some of your concern about the outcome of things. Grief can be, in time, liberating artistically. Because what's the worst that can happen?

You get a bad review?

Speaking of boldness, the work you made following Arthur's death feels so vast and singular, in terms of both its musicality and its risk-taking. In the book, you talk about "Ghosteen," your 2019 album, as an invented place where Arthur can perhaps find some sort of haven or rest: "I feel him roaming around the songs." But you're insistent that you don't mean this metaphorically—you mean it literally.

Things are a little different now than they were when I was making "Ghosteen." I was inside—deep inside—my grief. There were all manner of things that seemed possible in that space. I don't reject those feelings at all. In the book, I call it the impossible realm, which is not the imagination—it's adjacent to the imagination and in close proximity to death. It's a place where one has a sharpened awareness of the essentialness of things, and of the divine. I had a very real feeling at that time that I could help Arthur's spiritual condition—which really worried me—by creating beautiful music to surround him with. It upsets me when people wave this kind of thinking away as if it's just magical thinking, as if it's intellectually dishonest. Because these things helped me enormously. I would put religion in there, as well—religion can be extraordinarily helpful to people. I have a lot of time for religion, in all sorts of ways, but especially in the sense that it is a lifeline to people who really need it. There's an idea that religion is just a crutch—this is true, actually. Religion is a crutch, and a much-needed one. And I find the radical atheist idea of kicking out the crutches from under people with rationality is mean-spirited. That point of view—I hear it a lot. It feels unkind, ungenerous, inhumane.

You have also talked about "Ghosteen" as a way of reaching Arthur and saying goodbye. I think this is a feeling shared by people who have lost someone suddenly and violently—a need to make a different sort of ending. Yet was there any part of you that remained resistant to the idea of saying goodbye?

I'm not so sure I need to say goodbye anymore. It doesn't really work, anyway. [Laughs.] It's not like by saying goodbye the intimated presence of your lost ones wave to you and disappear. They're all around. And this is O.K. I think this is quite a beautiful thing. Everyone kept telling me that Arthur lived in my heart. Everyone said that, all the time.

I've heard that, too.

Yes, I'm sure you have. I never really understood that. I was once told by a very clever person to take Arthur out of my heart and put him by my side. This was the simplest notion, but extremely effective. For some time, he was just there, you know, beside me, as a spiritual companion. I would, in my way, discuss things with him. There was an actual relationship that went on, Arthur parenting me in my distress. I felt protected and emboldened by his presence. I don't do that sort of thing so much anymore, though those who have died are always in my prayers. But I don't feel that need in the same way as I did before. That's not to say that Susie and I don't capsize regularly. But we don't have that same terrible need.

People harden around the absence of a person they loved who has passed on. There's a deification of this absence. I think this is an extremely problematic situation to get yourself into, and it's not uncommon—living your life inwardly, focussing in on the dead rather than focussing outwardly on life and living. It's a difficult thing to negotiate early on. But it's essential that that happens. It can be difficult and sad, because it is the kind of letting go that no one wants to do. But necessary.

Well, it's another loss. A generative loss, maybe, but another loss.

Yes, but we do need to release the spirits of those who have passed on.

I have found myself more interested in ritual—lighting candles, things like that—as a way of giving space and physicality to what I'm feeling. Do you engage in any rituals, and have they been useful?

Well, yes, we must tend to ourselves as best we can. Personally, I go to church, which is in part ritual. A way of bringing these feelings, which are often so at odds with our ordinary, daily lives, and situating them within an institution that has been around for millennia and deals precisely in these matters—feelings of loss and spiritual yearning and regeneration—I drag in all my doubts and skepticisms and, on a good day, feel them lifted from me. This feeling of "laying one's burdens down" is extremely helpful, I find.

I think in the aftermath of loss there is a desire to transmute the grief somehow, to turn it into something else. Do you think that's what you've been doing? Transforming grief into performance, into art, as a way of both understanding and controlling it?

That's a lovely question. I haven't really thought of performance in that way. But, yes, you know, you are right, because grief is a condition of being, and there is not much room for its expression in the secular world. Performance, making art, using the imagination—I personally see these as non-secular acts. They are places, like grief, where we are transformed. Just to say, my audience has helped me enormously in that respect. Their regard, their concern has been overwhelming. As you say, a balm.

ERIS

265 Riverside Dr.
New York, NY 10025

This text was originally published as "Nick Cave on the Fragility of Life" by Amanda Petrusich in *The New Yorker* on March 23, 2023, and is republished here with permission from *The New Yorker*.

ISBN 978-1-967751-73-0

eris.press

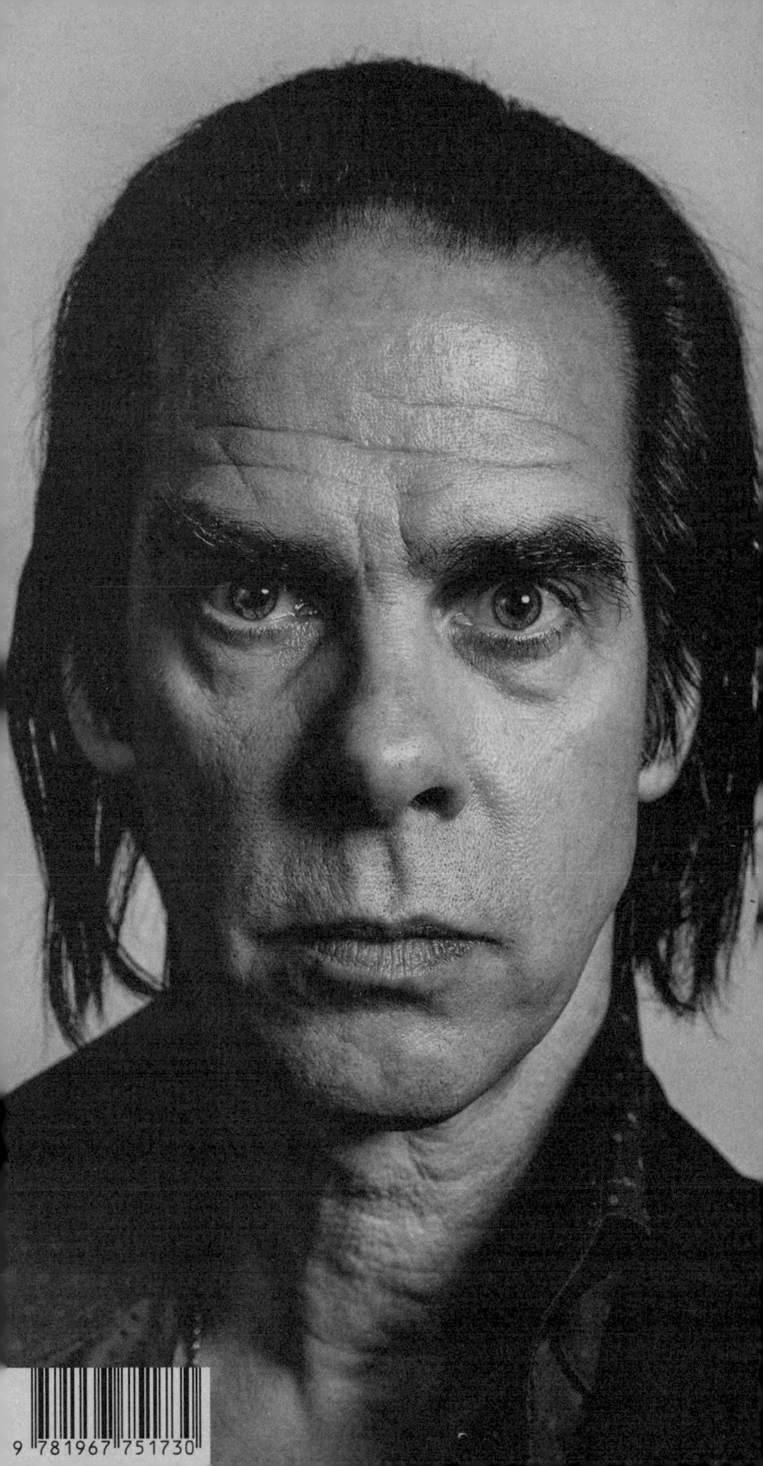
9 781967 751730